Ephesus

Colossae

Crete

D1796157

Hodder & Stoughton Bible Albums No. 10

PAUL, WITNESS TO THE GOSPEL

Editorial Committee
Father René Berthier
Jeanne-Marie Faure
Marie-Hélène Sigaut

Illustrated by
Lizzie Napoli

Translated by
Jane Collins

British Library Cataloguing in Publication Data
Berthier, René
   Paul, witness to the Gospel. – (Hodder and Stoughton
   Bible albums; vol. 10).
   1. Paul, *Saint* – Juvenile literature
   I. Title   II. Faure, Jeanne-Marie
   III. Sigaut, Marie-Hélène
   225.9'24   BS2506.5

   ISBN 0-340-25335-5

First published 1980
Original text and illustrations © 1979 by Univers-Media
English translation © 1980 by Hodder and Stoughton Ltd.

Printed in Belgium for Hodder and Stoughton Ltd.,
Mill Road, Dunton Green, Sevenoaks, Kent by
Henri Proost & Cie, Turnhout.

The text at the end of this volume is reproduced from the
New International Version of the Bible © 1978 by
New York International Bible Society,
published by Hodder & Stoughton.

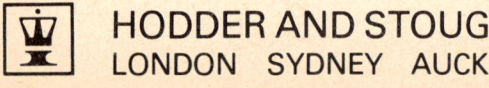

HODDER AND STOUGHTON
LONDON   SYDNEY   AUCKLAND   TORONTO

IN MAY 58 A.D., PAUL WAS ON HIS WAY TO JERUSALEM, BRINGING GIFTS FROM THE COMMUNITIES IN GREECE TO THE CHRISTIANS THERE. HE ARRIVED AT CAESAREA WITH HIS TRAVELLING COMPANIONS WHERE HE WAS WELCOMED BY PHILIP, ONE OF THE FIRST DEACONS. BY THIS TIME, PAUL WAS ABOUT FIFTY YEARS OLD.

5

PAUL AND HIS COMPANIONS STAYED WITH ONE OF PHILIP'S FRIENDS. THE NEXT DAY THEY WENT TO JAMES' HOUSE, WHERE ALL THE ELDERS OF THE JERUSALEM CHURCH WERE GATHERED.

Greetings, brothers. All the Christians in the Greek churches send their regards and ask you to accept this money as a sign of their love in Christ.

Thank you. By helping us in this way they show that their faith is real.

SO PAUL TOLD THEM IN DETAIL WHAT GOD HAD DONE AMONG THE GREEKS.

You've done some amazing work there, Paul. Let us thank God.

There are thousands of Jews who believe in Christ too. You'll see what we mean here.

But we've been hearing rumours about you.

It seems from what we've heard that you tell Jews who become Christians to stop following Jewish laws.

6

Some men are horrified. And quite rightly. If someone believes in Jesus but lives like a pagan, his faith is no good at all.

The Jewish religion can be summed up in one law which we must still keep: "Love your neighbour." From this it follows that he who loves is a friend of God.

THE ELDERS MADE A SUGGESTION TO PAUL. FOUR JEWS HAD TAKEN A VOW, AND TO BE RELEASED THEY WOULD HAVE TO PERFORM SPECIAL RITES IN THE TEMPLE. WOULD PAUL JOIN THEM AND PAY FOR THEIR SACRIFICES?

That way everyone will see you respect the law and stop criticizing you.

I'll do it if it will calm their fears. But you'll see I'm right in the end.

I was expecting a cool reception, but not this kind of haggling.

FOR SEVEN DAYS RUNNING, PAUL WENT TO THE TEMPLE AND CARRIED OUT THE RITES CAREFULLY.

7

ON THE SEVENTH DAY, SOME JEWS FROM THE PROVINCE OF ASIA RECOGNIZED PAUL.

THEY DRAGGED PAUL OUT OF THE TEMPLE TO KILL HIM.

THE TRIBUNE (THE ROMAN MILITARY COMMANDER) WAS INFORMED IMMEDIATELY. HE ORDERED HIS TROOPS TO BREAK UP THE CROWD.

PAUL TOLD THEM HOW, AS AN ARDENT ENEMY OF THE CHRISTIANS, HE HAD PERSECUTED THEM. THEN, ON THE ROAD TO DAMASCUS, JESUS HAD REVEALED HIMSELF TO HIM AND COMPLETELY TRANSFORMED HIS LIFE.
HE CONTINUED:

One day I was praying here, in the temple. And the Lord Jesus said to me, "Leave Jerusalem, for they will not accept your testimony. Go, I am sending you far away to the pagan nations."

You heard him that time: he really is against his people, against us!

Wipe him off the face of the earth!

He shouldn't be allowed to live!

Kill him!

THE NEXT DAY, THE TRIBUNE SUMMONED A MEETING OF THE SANHEDRIN (THE RELIGIOUS LEADERS OF ISRAEL) TO JUDGE PAUL.

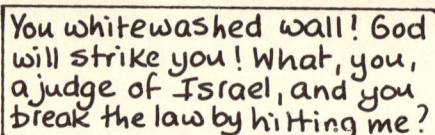

PAUL DEFENDED HIMSELF SKILFULLY. AWARE OF THE QUARRELS BETWEEN THE PHARISEES AND THE SADDUCEES, HE PLAYED ONE GROUP OFF AGAINST THE OTHER, UNTIL THEY STARTED FIGHTING AMONG THEMSELVES.

THE HEARING WAS ADJOURNED. THE SOLDIERS TOOK PAUL BACK TO THE BARRACKS.

PAUL'S NEPHEW HEARD RUMOURS OF THE PLOT AND WARNED HIS UNCLE.

Thank you for this news. Please send my love to your mother.

Take this young man to the tribune. He has something to report.

What have you to say?

The Jews have planned to ambush Paul. Don't allow him to be summoned, I beg you.

AND PAUL'S NEPHEW TOLD THE TRIBUNE ALL HE KNEW ABOUT THE PLOT.

Promise you won't tell anyone that you gave me this information.

Get ready 200 soldiers, 70 horsemen and a horse for Paul. You will leave for Caesarea at 9.00 tonight.

Write this letter: "I Claudius Lysias, the tribune, greet His Excellency, Governor Felix..."

IN HIS LETTER, THE TRIBUNE EXPLAINED TO THE GOVERNOR WHY HE WAS HAVING PAUL MOVED. HIS ORDERS WERE CARRIED OUT WITHOUT A HITCH.

GOVERNOR FELIX WAITED FOR PAUL'S ACCUSERS TO ARRIVE BEFORE BEGINNING THE TRIAL. THE HIGH PRIEST BROUGHT WITH HIM A LAWYER CALLED TERTULLUS.

Your Excellency, we know you to be a wise ruler and render our heartfelt gratitude to you. This man is a nuisance. He's causing trouble throughout the Jewish world. He's one of the leaders of the Nazarene sect. Among other things he has tried to profane the temple, and that's why we arrested him.

19

IN THE AUTUMN OF 60 A.D., PAUL WAS DELIVERED TO THE CENTURION JULIUS TO BE ESCORTED TO ROME. LUKE AND A DISCIPLE FROM THESSALONICA WENT WITH HIM.

THE BAD WEATHER PERSISTED, AND THE BOAT FELL BEHIND SCHEDULE. AT THE BEGINNING OF NOVEMBER, THEY WERE ONLY PASSING CRETE. AGAINST PAUL'S ADVICE, THEY DECIDED TO CARRY ON, BUT THEY HAD HARDLY REACHED OPEN SEA WHEN A GREAT STORM BROKE OUT.

THE STORM RAGED ON. FOR FOURTEEN DAYS THE SHIP WAS DRIVEN ALONG, HELPLESS.

We'll never get out of this alive.

The gods alone know where we are now. We can't even see the sun or stars to guide us.

If only we had listened to you! We shouldn't have left Crete. Too late now.

Don't be afraid. Not one of us will die. Only the boat will be lost. Pull yourselves together: eat and gain some strength – you'll need it!

AT LAST, AT DAWN ON THE FIFTEENTH DAY:

Land!

I don't recognize that coast. Where are we?

THEY ALL JUMPED INTO THE WATER AND ARRIVED SAFELY ON THE BEACH.

PAUL WAS ALLOWED TO HAVE PRIVATE LIVING QUARTERS. HE COULD HAVE VISITORS, AS LONG AS HE WAS HANDCUFFED TO A GUARD. AT FIRST, MOSTLY JEWS CAME TO SEE HIM, THEN OTHER PEOPLE.

Can you help me, Paul? In my community the others never let me have my say.

Do you love them sincerely? Do you show them that you do?

But after all, I'm a Roman patrician! I deserve some consideration!

So do the others. They deserve the same treatment as you. Never look down on them.

If they don't respect my rank, I shall lose all my privileges.

Don't seek your own interest: seek theirs. Try to have the attitude of Christ Jesus: he was equal to God, but renounced his privileges to become man, and a servant at that. He humbled himself to the extent of dying on a cross. That's why God raised him up above all things, and made him King and Lord.

ONE DAY, A SLAVE CAME TO SEEK REFUGE WITH PAUL.

Who are you? Why are you in such a state?

Save me, please!

He's shaking with fever. Luke, you're a doctor. Here's a chance to use your skill.

Now tell me your story. You have nothing to fear from me.

I've come from Colossae, in Asia. I am a slave of Philemon.

I've heard nothing but good about this Christian brother. You've left him?

He's not a bad master, but I don't want to be a slave any more. I can't stand not being free.

You know what you're risking now, if you're caught?

Yes, I'll die on a cross! You won't hand me over, will you?

No, of course not. You can stay here with us. We won't tell anyone.

I won't either. Listening to you, Paul, I want to be a Christian too.

PAUL ALSO RECEIVED OTHER MESSENGERS, BRINGING HIM NEWS OF THE VARIOUS COMMUNITIES.

Aquila, Priscilla, my dear friends!

How sad to see you in such a state.

I have learnt to find joy in my sufferings. The brothers gain strength because I am here, and I become more like Christ, helping to deliver the world from evil.

The brothers from Ephesus send their deep love. But there are serious problems there.

Some of them claim that there are "heavenly powers", and that we can only find God through them. They are getting bogged down in impossible intellectual arguments.

But that means they don't believe that Christ can lead us to God!

I've come from Colossae, and I can back up what they're saying. These empty discussions are the rage all over the region.

The elders are doing what they can. But it would be helpful if you could put them straight.

We'll come and see you again before we leave.

PAUL SPENT MUCH TIME PRAYING, THINKING, PREACHING THE GOSPEL, ENCOURAGING THE BROTHERS... HE GREW CLOSER AND CLOSER TO THE MYSTERY OF GOD, AND EXPRESSED IT AS BEST HE COULD...

Jesus, the visible image of the invisible God, is the first over all creation.

Everything was created by him and for him, invisible beings as well as visible.
Everything is sustained by him.
The Church is his body.
He is its head.
The fulness of God lives in him.
He makes peace through his blood and reconciles everything to himself by giving his life on the cross.

I've been making notes as we travelled, Paul. I think they may be useful one day.

I am sure that the Spirit of God is inspiring you, Luke. Christians in later times will be amazed at the power of the gospel, which has spread so far in so little time.

But there are important gaps in the notes. For example, the growth of the church in Corinth and Ephesus. I wasn't there myself...

SO PAUL TOLD HIM. TEN OR SO YEARS LATER LUKE WOULD WRITE THE SECOND PART OF THE ACTS OF THE APOSTLES.

WHILE HE WAS STAYING WITH PAUL, PHILEMON'S SLAVE BECAME A CHRISTIAN. PAUL GREW VERY FOND OF HIM, BUT HIS MASTER ASKED FOR HIM BACK.

Tell me, youngster, would you go back to your master now?

I would find it difficult to leave. You've become a father to me. But I see now that in the sight of our father in heaven, a master and his slave are equal. That helps.

I shall write to Philemon that he is to treat you like a brother, as if you were me. After all, aren't you my son in the faith?

I've seen the way you live: even in prison you've free.

A slave is free too, if the love of God rules in his heart.

I agree. But shouldn't a Christian master free his slaves when they become his brothers?

When I write to Philemon I shall ask him to do that for you.

ANOTHER DAY:

We would like to tell you what we feel, Paul. We are bound together by a deep love. My wife is so close to me that she seems to be part of me.

We feel as though we are swept off our feet by a greater love: that of God. Does that make sense?

Yes. That love is so great because it is the love of Christ.

He loved his church and gave himself for it. It has become his body. You are a living picture of that mystery.

ALTHOUGH BOUND IN PRISON,
PAUL'S SOUL SOARED FREE. HE
UNDERSTOOD NOW THAT GOD'S PLAN
OF LOVE WAS FOR ALL MEN,
WHEREVER OR WHENEVER THEY LIVE.

Blessed be God,
the Father of our Lord Jesus Christ.
From the beginning of time he
chose us to live in his presence,
in love.

Before we loved him he adopted
us as sons,
because of Jesus Christ
who frees us from all evil.

His great and loving plan was this:
to unite all men in Christ, who
can bring them back to life.

We who believe
are the witnesses of this hope.
The Holy Spirit who has been given
to us is like a deposit guaranteeing
our inheritance.

To bring this plan nearer to completion
is to give glory to God.

THE JEWISH LEADERS NEVER CAME TO ROME TO STATE THEIR CASE AGAINST PAUL, SO AFTER THE STATUTORY PERIOD, HE WAS FREED.

So you're free at last, Paul. It must be wonderful for you.

Yes, I thank God for it.

Where are you going to preach now?

I'm torn two ways: I want to go to Spain, but also back to Greece and Asia.

Can't you do both?

I'm not so young now. But I'm still running towards the goal. Straining with all my might, I'm looking forward to meeting face to face the Christ who set me on this path.

Thank you for all your support. May the love and peace of Christ be with you, Clement, and with all of you. Farewell.

NEXT DAY IN THE STREETS...

NERO HAD A GREAT NUMBER OF CHRISTIANS ARRESTED. THEY DIED UNDER TORTURE, IN THE ARENA, OR WERE USED AS BURNING TORCHES TO LIGHT UP THE EMPEROR'S GARDEN.

THE APOSTLE PETER HIMSELF GAVE HIS LIFE IN ROME AS A WITNESS TO HIS LOVE FOR CHRIST.

Yes. I'm a Christian, and I'm not ashamed of calling myself one. I thank God for it!

This time, Lord Jesus, I will not abandon and deny you. At last I can say to you truthfully, "You know that I love you."

PETER DIED IN ROME. THE BROTHERS BURIED THE APOSTLE THERE.

DURING THOSE YEARS, PAUL RETURNED TO EPHESUS. WHEN HE LEFT, HE HANDED THE CHURCH OVER TO TIMOTHY, LAYING HANDS ON HIM TO 'MAKE HIM A BISHOP.

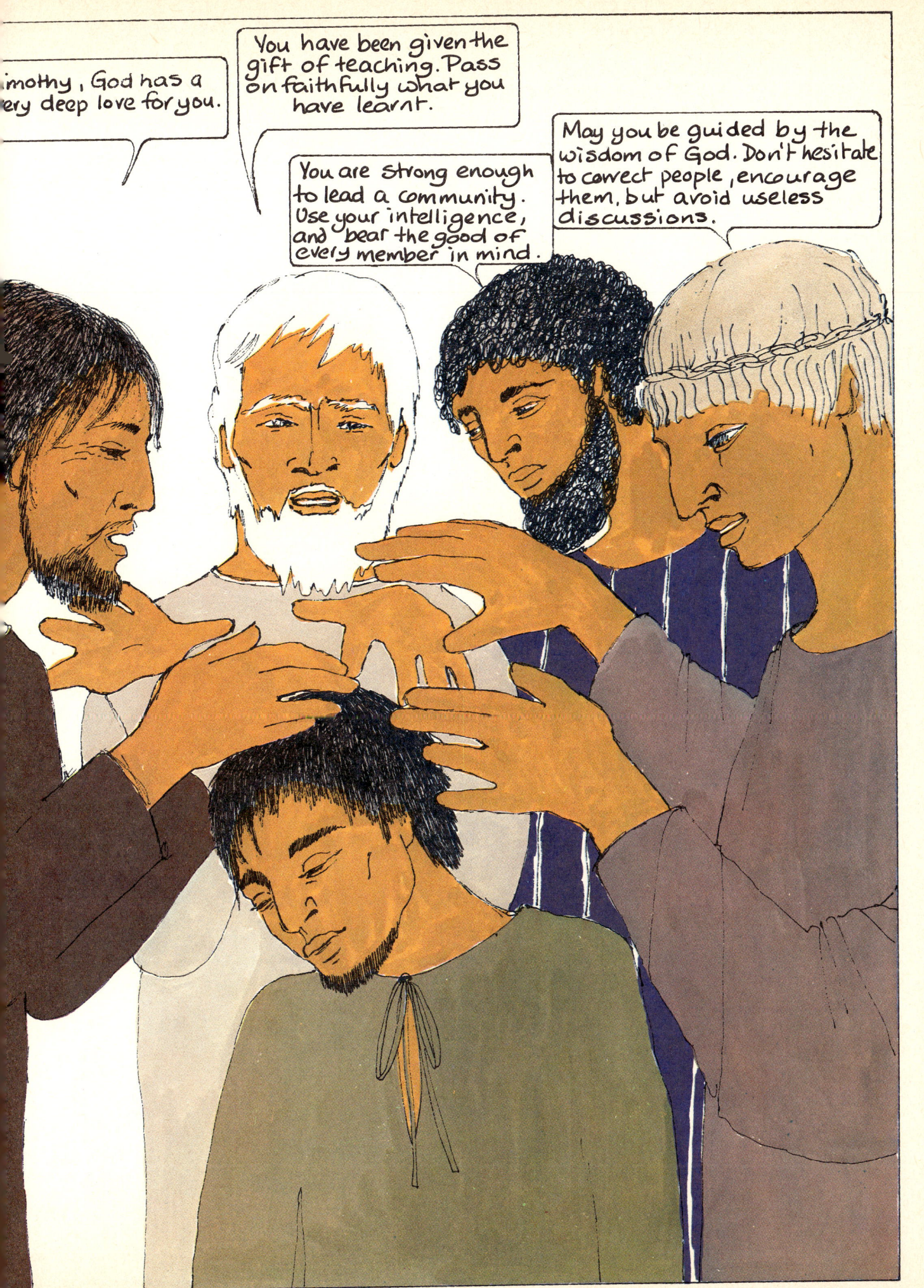

40

IN 67 PAUL WAS ARRESTED AGAIN. WHY? WE DON'T KNOW. ONCE MORE HE WAS TAKEN TO ROME. THIS TIME, PRISON LIFE WAS TOUGHER.

Here I am, chained up like a common criminal. Like you, Lord, before your passion.

I've already presented my case to the court once, but no one backed me up. They have all abandoned me. As they abandoned you...

I remember Jesus Christ, who was raised from the dead.

If we die with him, we shall live with him. If we suffer with him, we shall reign with him.

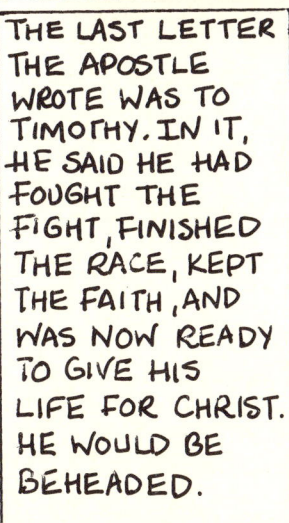

THE LAST LETTER THE APOSTLE WROTE WAS TO TIMOTHY. IN IT, HE SAID HE HAD FOUGHT THE FIGHT, FINISHED THE RACE, KEPT THE FAITH, AND WAS NOW READY TO GIVE HIS LIFE FOR CHRIST. HE WOULD BE BEHEADED.

Lord, it is in your power to do more for us than we can ask or think. Please, grant me to enter now into the fulness of your life.

FROM THAT TIME ON, CHRISTIANS ALL OVER THE WORLD HAVE CONTINUED TO LIVE BY THE WORD OF GOD.

Anything you do for the least of my brothers, you do it for me.
(Gospel of Matthew)

All creation is waiting in eager expectation to share in the glorious freedom of the children of God.
(Paul's letter to the Romans)

He came to give us life and life in all its fulness.
(Gospel of John)

Passages from the New Testament

which have inspired this book

The text is taken from the NEW INTERNATIONAL VERSION of the Bible.

Paul arrives in Caesarea

Acts 21:7-16   page 3

7 We continued our voyage from Tyre and landed at Ptolemais, where we greeted the brothers and stayed with them for a day. **8** Leaving the next day, we reached Caesarea and stayed at the house of Philip the evangelist, one of the Seven. **9** He had four unmarried daughters who had the gift of prophecy.

10 After we had been there a number of days, a prophet named Agabus came down from Judea. **11** Coming over to us, he took Paul's belt, tied his own hands and feet with it and said, "The Holy Spirit says, 'In this way the Jews of Jerusalem will bind the owner of this belt and will hand him over to the Gentiles.'"

12 When we heard this, we and the people there pleaded with Paul not to go up to Jerusalem. **13** Then Paul answered, "Why are you weeping and breaking my heart? I am ready not only to be bound, but also to die in Jerusalem for the name of the Lord Jesus." **14** When he would not be dissuaded, we gave up and said, "The Lord's will be done."

15 After this, we got ready and went up to Jerusalem. **16** Some of the disciples from Caesarea accompanied us and brought us to the home of Mnason, where we were to stay. He was a man from Cyprus and one of the early disciples.

Meeting with the elders in Jerusalem

Acts 21:17-25   page 6

17 When we arrived at Jerusalem, the brothers received us warmly. **18** The next day Paul and the rest of us went to see James and all the elders were present. **19** Paul greeted them and reported in detail what God had done among the Gentiles through his ministry.

20 When they heard this, they praised God. Then they said to Paul: "You see, brother, how many thousands of Jews have believed, and all of them are zealous for the law. **21** They have been informed that you teach all the Jews who live among the Gentiles to turn away from Moses, telling them not to circumcize their children or live according to our customs. **22** What shall we do? They will certainly hear that you have come, **23** so do what we tell you. There are four men with us who have made a vow. **24** Take these men, join in their purification rites and pay their expenses, so that they can have their heads shaved. Then everybody will know there is no truth in these reports about you, but that you yourself are living in obedience to the law. **25** As for the Gentile believers, we have written to them our decision that they should abstain from food sacrificed to idols, from blood, from the meat of strangled animals and from sexual immorality."

James 2:14-17

14 What good is it, my brothers, if a man claims to have faith but has no deeds? Can such faith save him? **15** Suppose a brother or sister is without clothes and daily food. **16** If one of you says to him, "Go, I wish you well; keep warm and well fed," but does nothing about his physical needs, what good is it? **17** In the same way, faith by itself, if it is not accompanied by action, is dead.

Romans 13:8, 10

8 Let no debt remain outstanding, except the continuing debt to love one another, for he who loves his fellow man has fulfilled the law.

10 Love does no harm to its neighbour. Therefore love is the fulfilment of the law.

Paul arrested in Jerusalem

Acts 21:26-36   pages 7, 8

26 The next day Paul took the men and purified himself along with them. Then he went to the temple to give notice of the date when the days of purification would end and the offering would be made for each of them.

27 When the seven days were nearly over, some Jews from the province of Asia saw Paul at the temple. They stirred up the whole crowd and seized him, **28** shouting, "Men of Israel, help us! This is the man who teaches all men everywhere against our people and our law and this place. And besides, he has brought Greeks into the temple area and defiled this holy place." **29** (They had previously seen Trophimus the Ephesian in the city with Paul and assumed that Paul had brought him into the temple area.)

30 The whole city was aroused, and the people came running from all directions. Seizing Paul, they dragged him from the temple, and immediately the gates were shut. **31** While they were trying to kill him, news reached the commander of the Roman troops that the whole city of Jerusalem was in an uproar. **32** He at once took some officers and soldiers and ran down to the crowd. When the rioters saw the commander and his soldiers, they stopped beating Paul.

33 The commander came up and arrested him and ordered him to be bound with two chains. Then he asked who he was and what he had done. **34** Some in the crowd shouted one thing and some another, and since the commander could not get at the truth because of the uproar, he ordered that Paul be taken into the barracks. **35** When Paul reached the steps, the violence of the mob was so great he had to be carried by the soldiers. **36** The crowd that followed kept shouting, "Away with him!"

Paul speaks to the crowd

Acts 21:37–22:5, 17, 18, 21-24   page 9

37 As the soldiers were about to take Paul into the barracks, he asked the commander, "May I say something to you?"

"Do you speak Greek?" he replied. **38** "Aren't you the Egyptian who started a revolt and led four thousand terrorists out into the desert some time ago?"

39 Paul answered, "I am a Jew, from Tarsus in Cilicia, a citizen of no ordinary city. Please let me speak to the people."

40 Having received the commander's permission, Paul stood on the steps and motioned to the crowd. When they were all silent, he said to them in Aramaic: **1** "Brothers and fathers, listen now to my defence." **2** When they heard him speak to them in Aramaic, they became very quiet.

Then Paul said: **3** "I am a Jew, born in Tarsus of Cilicia, but brought up in this city. Under Gamaliel I was thoroughly trained in the law of our fathers and was just as zealous for God as any of you are today. **4** I persecuted the followers of this Way to their death, arresting both men and women and throwing them into prison, 5 as also the high priest and all the council can testify. I even obtained letters from them to their brothers in Damascus, and went there to bring these people as prisoners to Jerusalem to be punished. . . .

(*Paul tells the story of his conversion*)

17 "When I returned to Jerusalem and was praying at the temple, I fell into a trance 18 and saw the Lord speaking. 'Quick!' he said to me. 'Leave Jerusalem immediately, because they will not accept your testimony about me.'

21 "Then the Lord said to me, 'Go; I will send you far away to the Gentiles.'"

22 The crowd listened to Paul until he said this. Then they raised their voices and shouted, "Rid the earth of him! He's not fit to live!"

23 As they were shouting and throwing off their cloaks and flinging dust into the air, 24 the commander ordered Paul to be taken into the barracks. He directed that he be flogged and questioned in order to find out why the people were shouting at him like this.

Paul, the Roman citizen
Acts 22:25-29   page 11

25 As they stretched him out to flog him, Paul said to the centurion standing there, "Is it legal for you to flog a Roman citizen who hasn't even been found guilty?"

26 When the centurion heard this, he went to the commander and reported it. "What are you going to do?" he asked. "This man is a Roman citizen."

27 The commander went to Paul and asked, "Tell me, are you a Roman citizen?"

"Yes, I am," he answered.

28 Then the commander said, "I had to pay a big price for my citizenship."

"But I was born a citizen," Paul replied.

29 Those who were about to question him withdrew immediately. The commander himself was alarmed when he realized that he had put Paul, a Roman citizen, in chains.

Before the Sanhedrin
Acts 22:30–23:11   page 12

30 The next day, since the commander wanted to find out exactly why Paul was being accused by the Jews, he released him and ordered the chief priests and all the Sanhedrin to assemble. Then he brought Paul and had him stand before them.

1 Paul looked straight at the Sanhedrin and said, "My brothers, I have fulfilled my duty to God in all good conscience to this day." 2 At this the high priest Ananias ordered those standing near to Paul to strike him on the mouth. 3 Then Paul said to him, "God will strike you, you whitewashed wall! You sit there to judge me according to the law, yet you yourself violate the law by commanding that I be struck!"

4 Those who were standing near Paul said, "You dare to insult God's high priest?"

5 Paul replied, "Brothers, I did not realise that he was the high priest; for it is written: 'Do not speak evil about the ruler of your people.'"

6 Then Paul, knowing that some of them were Sadducees and the others Pharisees, called out in the Sanhedrin, "My brothers, I am a Pharisee, the son of a Pharisee. I stand on trial because of my hope in the resurrection of the dead." 7 When he said this, a dispute broke out between the Pharisees and the Sadducees, and the assembly was divided. 8 (The Sadducees say that there is no resurrection, and that there are neither angels nor spirits, but the Pharisees acknowledge them all.)

9 There was a great uproar, and some of the teachers of the law who were Pharisees stood up and argued vigorously. "We find nothing wrong with this man," they said.

"What if a spirit or an angel has spoken to him?" 10 The dispute became so violent that the commander was afraid Paul would be torn to pieces by them. He ordered the troops to go down and take him away from them by force and bring him into the barracks.

11 The following night the Lord stood near Paul and said, "Take courage! As you have testified about me in Jerusalem, so you must also testify in Rome."

The plot to kill Paul
Acts 23:12-22   pages 13, 14

12 The next morning the Jews formed a conspiracy and bound themselves with an oath not to eat or drink until they had killed Paul. 13 More than forty men were involved in this plot. 14 They went to the chief priests and elders and said, "We have taken a solemn oath not to eat anything until we have killed Paul. 15 Now then, you and the Sanhedrin petition the commander to bring him before you on the pretext of wanting more accurate information about his case. We are ready to kill him before he gets here."

16 But when the son of Paul's sister heard of this plot, he went into the barracks and told Paul.

17 Then Paul called one of the centurions and said, "Take this young man to the commander; he has something to tell him." 18 So he took him to the commander.

The centurion said, "Paul, the prisoner, sent for me and asked me to bring this young man to you because he has something to tell you."

19 The commander took the young man by the hand, drew him aside and asked, "What is it you want to tell me?"

20 He said: "The Jews have agreed to ask you to bring Paul before the Sanhedrin tomorrow on the pretext of wanting more accurate information about him. 21 Don't give in to them, because more than forty of them are waiting in ambush for him. They have taken an oath not to eat or drink until they have killed him. They are ready now, waiting for your consent to their request."

22 The commander dismissed the young man and cautioned him, "Don't tell anyone that you have reported this to me."

Paul transferred to Caesarea
Acts 23:23-35   page 14

23 Then he called two of his centurions and ordered them, "Get ready a detachment of two hundred soldiers, seventy horsemen and two hundred spearmen to go to Caesarea at nine tonight. 24 Provide mounts for Paul so that he may be taken safely to Governor Felix."

25 He wrote a letter as follows:

26 Claudius Lysias,

To his Excellency, Governor Felix:

Greetings.

27 This man was seized by the Jews and they were about to kill him, but I came with my troops and rescued him, for I had learned that he is a Roman citizen. 28 I wanted to know why they were accusing him, so I brought him to their Sanhedrin. 29 I found that the accusation had to do with questions about their law, but there was no charge against him that deserved death or imprisonment. 30 When I was informed of a plot to be carried out against the man, I sent him to you at once. I also ordered his accusers to present to you their case against him.

31 So the soldiers, carrying out their orders, took Paul with them during the night and brought him as far as Antipatris. 32 The next day they let the cavalry go on with him, while they returned to the barracks. 33 When the

cavalry arrived in Caesarea, they delivered the letter to the governor and handed Paul over to him. 34 The governor read the letter and asked what province he was from. Learning that he was from Cilicia, 35 he said, "I will hear your case when your accusers get here." Then he ordered that Paul be kept under guard in Herod's palace.

Ephesians 6:19, 20 page 15

19 Pray also for me, that whenever I open my mouth, words may be given me so that I will fearlessly make known the mystery of the gospel, 20 for which I am an ambassador in chains. Pray that I may declare it fearlessly, as I should.

Acts 26:22

22 But I have had God's help to this very day, and so I stand here and testify to small and great alike.

The trial before Felix
Acts 24:1-13,19-22 page 16

1 Five days later the high priest Ananias went down to Caesarea with some of the elders and a lawyer named Tertullus, and they brought their charges against Paul before the governor. 2 When Paul was called in, Tertullus presented his case before Felix: "We have enjoyed a long period of peace under you, and your foresight has brought about reforms in this nation. 3 Everywhere and in every way, most excellent Felix, we acknowledge this with profound gratitude. 4 But in order not to weary you further, I would request that you be kind enough to hear us briefly.

5 "We have found this man to be a troublemaker, stirring up riots among the Jews all over the world. He is a ring-leader of the Nazarene sect 6 and even tried to desecrate the temple; so we seized him. 8 By examining him yourself you will be able to learn the truth about all these charges we are bringing against him."

9 The Jews joined in the accusation, asserting that these things were true.

10 When the governor motioned for him to speak, Paul replied: "I know that for a number of years you have been a judge over this nation; so I gladly make my defence. 11 You can easily verify that no more than twelve days ago I went up to Jerusalem to worship. 12 My accusers did not find me arguing with anyone at the temple, or stirring up a crowd in the synagogues or anywhere else in the city. 13 And they cannot prove to you the charges they are now making against me. . . .

19 But there are some Jews from the province of Asia, who ought to be here before you and bring charges if they have anything against me. 20 Or these who are here should state what crime they found in me when I stood before the Sanhedrin—21 unless it was this one thing I shouted as I stood in their presence. 'It is concerning the resurrection of the dead that I am on trial before you today.' "

22 Then Felix, who was well acquainted with the Way, adjourned the proceedings. "When Lysias the commander comes," he said, "I will decide your case."

Imprisoned in Caesarea
Acts 24:23-27 page 18

23 He ordered the centurion to keep Paul under guard but to give him some freedom and permit his friends to take care of his needs.

24 Several days later Felix came with his wife Drusilla, who was a Jewess. He sent for Paul and listened to him as he spoke about faith in Christ Jesus. 25 As Paul discoursed on righteousness, self-control and the judgment to come, Felix was afraid and said, "That's enough for now! You may leave. When I find it convenient, I will send for you."

26 At the same time he was hoping that Paul would offer him a bribe, so he sent for him frequently and talked with him.

27 When two years had passed, Felix was succeeded by Porcius Festus, but because Felix wanted to grant a favour to the Jews, he left Paul in prison.

Romans 9:3-5, 10:9, 12, 5:18-20

3 For I could wish that I myself were cursed and cut off from Christ for the sake of my brothers, those of my own race, 4 the people of Israel. Theirs is the adoption as sons; theirs the divine glory, the covenants, the receiving of the law, the temple worship and the promises. 5 Theirs are the patriarchs, and from them is traced the human ancestry of Christ, who is God over all, for ever praised! Amen.

9 If you confess with your mouth, "Jesus is Lord," and believe in your heart that God raised him from the dead, you will be saved.

12 For there is no difference between Jew and Gentile—the same Lord is Lord of all and richly blesses all who call on him.

18 Consequently, just as the result of one trespass was condemnation for all men, so also the result of one act of righteousness was justification that brings life for all men. 19 For just as through the disobedience of the one man the many were made sinners, so also through the obedience of the one man the many will be made righteous.

20 The law was added so that the trespass might increase. But where sin increased, grace increased all the more.

Paul appeals to Caesar
Acts 25:1-12 page 19

1 Three days after arriving in the province, Festus went up from Caesarea to Jerusalem, 2 where the chief priests and Jewish leaders appeared before him and presented the charges against Paul. 3 They urgently requested Festus, as a favour to them, to have Paul transferred to Jerusalem, for they were preparing an ambush to kill him along the way. 4 Festus answered, "Paul is being held at Caesarea, and I myself am going there soon. 5 Let some of your leaders come with me and press charges against the man there, if he has done anything wrong."

6 After spending eight or ten days with them, he went down to Caesarea, and the next day he convened the court and ordered that Paul be brought before him. 7 When Paul appeared, the Jews who had come down from Jerusalem stood around him, bringing many serious charges against him, which they could not prove.

8 Then Paul made his defence: "I have done nothing wrong against the law of the Jews or against the temple or against Caesar."

9 Festus, wishing to do the Jews a favour, said to Paul, "Are you willing to go up to Jerusalem and stand trial before me there on these charges?"

10 Paul answered: "I am now standing before Caesar's court, where I ought to be tried. I have not done any wrong to the Jews, as you yourself know very well. 11 If, however, I am guilty of doing anything deserving death, I do not refuse to die. But if the charges brought against me by these Jews are not true, no-one has the right to hand me over to them. I appeal to Caesar!"

12 After Festus had conferred with his council, he declared: "You have appealed to Caesar. To Caesar you will go!"

Paul before Agrippa
Acts 25:13, 14, 22, 23, 26:1, 27-32

13 A few days later King Agrippa and Bernice arrived at Caesarea to pay their respects to Festus. 14 Since they were spending many days there, Festus discussed Paul's case with the king. . . .

22 Then Agrippa said to Festus, "I would like to hear this man myself."...

23 The next day Agrippa and Bernice came with great pomp and entered the audience room with the high ranking officers and the leading men of the city. At the command of Festus, Paul was brought in....

1 Then Agrippa said to Paul, "You have permission to speak for yourself."

So Paul motioned with his hand and began his defence. (*Paul speaks of his conversion and his faith.*)

27 "King Agrippa, do you believe the prophets? I know you do."

28 Then Agrippa said to Paul, "Do you think that in such a short time you can persuade me to be a Christian?"

29 Paul replied, "Short time or long—I pray God that not only you but all who are listening to me today may become what I am, except for these chains."

30 The king rose, and with him the governor and Bernice and those sitting with them. **31** They left the room, and while talking with one another, they said, "This man is not doing anything that deserves death or imprisonment."

32 Agrippa said to Festus, "This man could have been set free, if he had not appealed to Caesar."

Paul sails for Rome
Acts 27:1, 7-12   page 21

1 When it was decided that we would sail for Italy, Paul and some other prisoners were handed over to a centurion named Julius....

7 We made slow headway for many days and had difficulty arriving off Cnidus. When the wind did not allow us to hold our course, we sailed to the lee of Crete, opposite Salmone. **8** We moved along the coast with difficulty and came to a place called Fair Havens, near the town of Lasea.

9 Much time had been lost, and sailing had already become dangerous because by now it was after the Fast. So Paul warned them, **10** "Men, I can see that our voyage is going to be disastrous and bring great loss to ship and cargo, and to our own lives also." **11** But the centurion, instead of listening to what Paul said, followed the advice of the pilot and of the owner of the ship. **12** Since the harbour was unsuitable to winter in, the majority decided that we should sail on, hoping to reach Phoenix and winter there.

Storm and shipwreck
Acts 27:13-22, 27, 33-37, 39, 41-44; 28:1, 2   pages 22-24

13 When a gentle south wind began to blow, they thought they had obtained what they wanted; so they weighed anchor and sailed along the shore of Crete. **14** Before very long, a wind of hurricane force, called the "North-easter", swept down from the island. **15** The ship was caught by the storm and could not head into the wind; so we gave way to it and were driven along. **16** As we passed to the lee of a small island called Cauda, we were hardly able to make the lifeboat secure. **17** When the men had hoisted it aboard, they passed ropes under the ship itself to hold it together. Fearing that they would run aground on the sand-bars of Syrtis, they lowered the sea anchor and let the ship be driven along. **18** We took such a violent battering from the storm that the next day they began to throw the cargo overboard. **19** On the third day, they threw the ship's tackle overboard with their own hands. **20** When neither sun nor stars appeared for many days and the storm continued raging, we finally gave up all hope of being saved.

21 After the men had gone a long time without food, Paul stood up before them and said: "Men, you should have taken my advice not to sail from Crete; then you would have spared yourselves this damage and loss. **22**

But now I urge you to keep up your courage, because not one of you will be lost; only the ship will be destroyed...."

27 On the fourteenth night we were still being driven across the Adriatic Sea, when about midnight the sailors sensed they were approaching land....

33 Just before dawn Paul urged them all to eat. "For the last fourteen days," he said, "you have been in constant suspense and have gone without food—you haven't eaten anything. **34** Now I urge you to take some food. You need it to survive. Not one of you will lose a single hair from his head." **35** After he said this, he took some bread and gave thanks to God in front of them all. Then he broke it and began to eat. **39** They were all encouraged and ate some food themselves. **37** Altogether there were two hundred and seventy-six of us on board....

39 When daylight came, they did not recognize the land, but they saw a bay with a sandy beach, where they decided to run the ship aground if they could....

41 But the ship struck a sand-bar and ran aground. The bow stuck fast and would not move, and the stern was broken to pieces by the pounding of the surf.

42 The soldiers planned to kill the prisoners to prevent any of them from swimming away and escaping. **43** But the centurion wanted to spare Paul's life and kept them from carrying out their plan. He ordered those who could swim to jump overboard first and get to land. **44** The rest were to get there on planks or on pieces of the ship. In this way everyone reached land in safety....

1 Once safely on shore, we found out that the island was called Malta. **2** The islanders showed us unusual kindness. They built a fire and welcomed us all because it was raining and cold.

Arrival at Rome
Acts 28:11-15   page 25

11 After three months we put out to sea in a ship that had wintered in the island....

12 We put in at Syracuse and stayed there three days. **13** From there we set sail and arrived at Rhegium. The next day the south wind came up, and on the following day we reached Puteoli. **14** There we found some brothers who invited us to spend a week with them. And so we went to Rome. **15** The brothers there had heard that we were coming, and they travelled as far as the Forum of Appius and the Three Taverns to meet us. At the sight of these men Paul thanked God and was encouraged.

A prisoner in Rome
Acts 28:16, 17, 30, 31   page 26

16 When we got to Rome, Paul was allowed to live by himself, with a soldier to guard him.

17 Three days later he called together the leaders of the Jews.

30 For two whole years Paul stayed there in his own rented house and welcomed all who came to see him. **31** Boldly and without hindrance he preached the kingdom of God and taught about the Lord Jesus Christ.

Have the attitude of Christ
Romans 12:10   page 26

10 Be devoted to one another in brotherly love. Honour one another above yourselves.

2 Make my joy complete by being like-minded, having the same love, being one in spirit and purpose. 3 Do nothing out of selfish ambition or vain conceit, but in humility consider others better than yourselves. 4 Each of you should look not only to your own interests, but also to the interests of others. 5 Your attitude should be the same as that of Christ Jesus:

6 Who, being in very nature
 God,
 did not consider equality
 with God
 something to be grasped,
7 but made himself nothing,
 taking the very nature of a
 servant,
 being made in human
 likeness.
8 And being found in
 appearance as a man,
 he humbled himself
 and became obedient to
 death—
 even death on a cross!
9 Therefore God exalted him to
 the highest place
 and gave him the name that
 is above every name,
10 that at the name of Jesus every
 knee should bow,
 in heaven and on earth and
 under the earth,
11 and every tongue confess that
 Jesus Christ is Lord,
 to the glory of God the
 Father.

Colossians 1:24   page 28

24 Now I rejoice in what was suffered for you, and I fill up in my flesh what is still lacking in regard to Christ's afflictions, for the sake of his body, which is the church.

Avoid deceptive philosophies

Colossians 2:8, 9, 16-18, 20-22   page 28

8 See to it that no-one takes you captive through hollow and deceptive philosophy, which depends on human tradition and the basic principles of this world rather than on Christ.
9 For in Christ all the fulness of the Deity lives in bodily form. . . .

16 Therefore do not let anyone judge you by what you eat or drink, or with regard to a religious festival, a new moon celebration or a Sabbath day. 17 These are a shadow of the things that were to come; the reality, however, is found in Christ. 18 Do not let anyone who delights in false humility and the worship of angels disqualify you for the prize. . . .

20 Since you died with Christ to the basic principles of this world, why, as though you still belonged to it, do you submit to its rules: 21 "Do not handle! Do not taste! Do not touch!"? 22 These are all destined to perish with use, because they are based on human commands and teachings.

Jesus, the image of God

Colossians 1:15-20   page 29

15 He is the image of the invisible God, the firstborn over all creation. 16 For by him all things were created: things in heaven and on earth, visible and invisible, whether thrones or powers or rulers or authorities; all things were created by him and for him. 17 He is before all things, and in him all things hold together. 18 And he is the head of the body, the church; he is the beginning and the firstborn from among the dead, so that in everything he might have the supremacy. 19 For God was pleased to have all his fulness dwell in him, 20 and through him to reconcile to himself all things, whether things on earth or things in heaven, by making peace through his blood, shed on the cross.

Paul's concern for a slave

Philemon 9,10,12,17-20,22   page 31

9 I then, as Paul—an old man and now also a prisoner of Christ Jesus—10 I appeal to you for my son Onesimus, who became my son while I was in chains. . . .

12 I am sending him—who is my very heart— back to you.

17 So if you consider me a partner, welcome him as you would welcome me. 18 If he has done you any wrong or owes you anything, charge it to me. 19 I, Paul, am writing this with my own hand. I will pay it back—not to mention that you owe me your very self. 20 I do wish, brother, that I may have some benefit from you in the Lord; refresh my heart in Christ. . . .

22 And one thing more: Prepare a guest room for me, because I hope to be restored to you in answer to your prayers.

Husbands, love your wives . . .

Ephesians 5:25-32   page 32

25 Husbands, love your wives, just as Christ loved the church and gave himself up for her 26 to make her holy, cleansing her by the washing with water through the word, 27 and to present her to himself as a radiant church, without stain or wrinkle or any other blemish, but holy and blameless. 28 In this same way, husbands ought to love their wives as their own bodies. He who loves his wife loves himself. 29 After all, no-one ever hated his own body, but he feeds and cares for it, just as Christ does the church—30 for we are members of his body. 31 "For this reason a man will leave his father and mother and be united to his wife, and the two will become one flesh." 32 This is a profound mystery—but I am talking about Christ and the church.

God's purpose

Ephesians 1:3-14   page 33

3 Praise be to the God and Father of our Lord Jesus Christ, who has blessed us in the heavenly realms with every spiritual blessing in Christ. 4 For he chose us in him before the creation of the world to be holy and blameless in his sight. In love 5 he predestined us to be adopted as his sons through Jesus Christ, in accordance with his pleasure and will—6 to the praise of his glorious grace, which he has freely given us in the One he loves. 7 In him we have redemption through his blood, the forgiveness of sins, in accordance with the riches of God's grace 8 that he lavished on us with all wisdom and understanding. And 9 he made known to us the mystery of his will according to his good pleasure, which he purposed in Christ, 10 to be put into effect when the times will have reached their fulfilment—to bring all things in heaven and on earth together under one head, even Christ.

11 In him we were also chosen, having been predestined according to the plan for him who works out everything in conformity with the purpose of his will, 12 in order that we, who were the first to hope in Christ, might be for the praise of his glory. 13 And you also were included in Christ when you heard the word of truth, the gospel of your salvation. Having believed, you were marked in him with a seal, the promised Holy Spirit, 14 who is a deposit guaranteeing our inheritance until the redemption of those who are God's possession—to the praise of his glory.

Paul's great aim in life
Philippians 3:10-14

10 I want to know Christ and the power of his resurrection and the fellowship of sharing in his sufferings, becoming like him in his death, 11 and so, somehow, to attain to the resurrection from the dead.

12 Not that I have already obtained all this, or have already been made perfect, but I press on to take hold of that for which Christ Jesus took hold of me. 13 Brothers, I do not consider myself yet to have taken hold of it. But one thing I do: Forgetting what is behind and straining towards what is ahead, 14 I press on towards the goal to win the prize for which God has called me heavenwards in Christ Jesus.

Advice to Timothy
1 Timothy 4:12-15; 3:1-4, 7, 8, 11; 5:1, 2; 2:1, 3, 4 page 38

12 Don't let anyone look down on you because you are young, but set an example for the believers in speech, in life, in love, in faith and in purity. 13 Until I come, devote yourself to the public reading of Scripture, to preaching and to teaching. 14 Do not neglect your gift, which was given you through a prophetic message when the body of elders laid their hands on you.

15 Be diligent in these matters. . . .

1 Here is a trustworthy saying: If anyone sets his heart on being an overseer (or bishop), he desires a noble task. 2 Now the overseer must be above reproach, the husband of but one wife, temperate, self-controlled, respectable, hospitable, able to teach, 3 not given to much wine, not violent but gentle, not quarrelsome, not a lover of money. 4 He must manage his own family well and see that his children obey him with proper respect. . . . 7 He must also have a good reputation with outsiders, so that he will not fall into disgrace and into the devil's trap.

8 Deacons, likewise, are to be men worthy of respect, sincere, not indulging in much wine, and not pursuing dishonest gain. . . .

11 In the same way, their wives are to be women worthy of respect, not malicious talkers but temperate and trustworthy in everything. . . .

1 Do not rebuke an older man harshly, but exhort him as if he were your father. Treat younger men as brothers, 2 older women as mothers, and younger women as sisters, with absolute purity. . . .

1 I urge, then, first of all, that requests, prayers, intercession and thanksgiving be made for everyone. . . .

3 This is good, and pleases God our Saviour, 4 who wants all men to be saved and to come to a knowledge of the truth.

Paul at the end of his life
2 Timothy 4:16; 2:8-12; 4:6-8 page 41

16 At my first defence, no-one came to my support, but everyone deserted me. May it not be held against them.

8 Remember Jesus Christ, raised from the dead, descended from David. This is my gospel, 9 for which I am suffering even to the point of being chained like a criminal. But God's word is not chained. 10 Therefore I endure everything for the sake of the elect, that they too may obtain the salvation that is in Christ Jesus, with eternal glory.

11 Here is a trustworthy saying:
If we died with him,
    we will also live with him;
12 if we endure,
    we will also reign with
    him.

6 For I am already being poured out like a drink offering, and the time has come for my departure. 7 I have fought the good fight, I have finished the race, I have kept the faith. 8 Now there is in store for me the crown of righteousness, which the Lord, the righteous Judge, will award to me on that day—and not only to me, but also to all who have longed for his appearing.

Ephesians 3:17-21

17 I pray that Christ may dwell in your hearts through faith. And I pray that you, being rooted and established in love, 18 may have power, together with all the saints, to grasp how wide and long and high and deep is the love of Christ, 19 and to know this love that surpasses knowledge—that you may be filled to the measure of all the fulness of God.

20 Now to him who is able to do immeasurably more than all we ask or imagine, according to his power that is at work within us, 21 to him be glory in the church and in Christ Jesus throughout all generations, for ever and ever! Amen.

Among the historical texts which have inspired us, the most significant is that by the Roman historian Tacitus, written towards A.D. 110 as part of his Annals of Imperial Rome. *It provides evidence for the existence of Christ and for the presence of a large Christian community in Rome itself. The information he offers is all the more important because Tacitus was not sympathetic to Christianity.*

"But neither human resources, nor imperial munificence, nor appeasement of the gods eliminated sinister suspicions that the fire had been instigated. To suppress this rumour, Nero fabricated scapegoats—and punished with every refinement the notoriously depraved Christians (as they were popularly called.) Their originator, Christ, had been executed in Tiberius' reign by the governor of Judea, Pontius Pilatus. But in spite of this temporary setback the deadly superstition had broken out afresh, not only in Judea (where the mischief had started) but even in Rome. All degraded and shameful practices collect and flourish in the capital.

"First, Nero had self-acknowledged Christians arrested. Then, on their information, large numbers of others were condemned—not so much for incendiarism as for their anti-social tendencies. Their deaths were made farcical. Dressed in wild animals' skins, they were torn to pieces by dogs, or crucified, or made into torches to be ignited after dark as substitutes for daylight. Nero provided his Gardens for the spectacle, and exhibited displays in the Circus, at which he mingled with the crowd—or stood in a chariot, dressed as a charioteer. Despite their guilt as Christians, and the ruthless punishment it deserved, the victims were pitied. For it was felt that they were being sacrificed to one man's brutality rather than to the national interest."

(*From* The Annals of Imperial Rome, *translated by Michael Grant, Penguin Books*)

PRINTED IN BELGIUM BY  proost INTERNATIONAL BOOK PRODUCTION